PUBLICATIONS

Why Isn't My Giving Working?

The Four Types of Giving

All Scripture quotations are from the King James Version of the Bible unless otherwise noted.

Scripture quotations marked (NKJV) are from New King James Version®. Copyright ©1982 by Thomas Nelson. Used by permission. All rights reserved.

Scripture quotations marked (NIV) are taken from the Holy Bible, New International Version®. NIV® Copyright © 1973, 1978, 1984, 2011, by Biblica, Inc.™ All rights reserved worldwide. www.zondervan.com The "NIV" and "New International Version" are trademarks registered in the United States Patent and Trademark Office by Biblica, Inc.™

Scripture quotations taken from the Amplified® Bible (AMPC),
Copyright © 1954, 1958, 1962, 1964, 1965, 1987 by The Lockman Foundation
Used by permission. www.Lockman.org

Why Isn't My Giving Working?
The Four Types of Giving
ISBN 978-0-9819977-3-5
Copyright © 2013 Jesse Duplantis
Published by Jesse Duplantis Ministries
8th Printing 2019

Jesse Duplantis Ministries
PO Box 1089
Destrehan, LA 70047
USA
www.jdm.org

Jesse Duplantis Ministries is dedicated to reaching people and changing lives with the Gospel of Jesus Christ. For more information or to purchase other products from Jesse Duplantis Ministries, please contact us at the address above.

Printed in the United States of America. All rights reserved under International Copyright Law. Contents and/or cover may not be reproduced in whole or in part in any form without the express written consent of the publisher.

Contents

Chapter One
The Four Types of Giving 7

Chapter Two
The Tithe 13

Chapter Three
Firstfruits 21

Chapter Four
Alms 27

Chapter Five
Seed 39

Chapter Six
Testimonies 55

Chapter One

The Four Types of Giving

What I'm about to share with you literally changed the way I thought about giving and, in turn, it changed the way I live my life when it comes to my giving. I was financially successful before I came to know the Lord, but because of how I was raised and everything I'd ever heard, when I accepted Jesus as my Savior, I wrongly assumed that I had to be poor to serve the Lord. So, I gave all my money away and started living life as a good Christian. I immediately began to tithe because I knew it was the right thing to do and, little by little, I came to find teachings and scriptures that began to enlighten me on God's way of getting something to His people.

Long after I'd become a minister of the Gospel and had a growing evangelistic ministry, God gave me a revelation about seed-sowing while jogging one day that totally changed my life. Out of that revelation, the message "Hey! That's My Harvest!" was born. It revolutionized the way I gave, and from the response I got from many others, it did the same for them. From that time until now, I have never looked back. I always believed in my heart that God wanted His people not to hurt, but to be joyful and blessed. But I have learned that God put principles in His Word to get us there.

It's exciting! This teaching is one that I use personally in my own giving, and I don't have to tell you…I'm a blessed man! I have never had a financial deficit in my 35 years of ministry. I am living proof that anyone can "Believe the Unbelievable and Receive the Impossible." I'm a Cajun from South Louisiana who was raised harshly, brought up poor, and indoctrinated with the man-made theory that poverty equals holiness. I can say without a shred of pride in myself that God has broken the shackles off of my life in every way—spiritually first, but also financially—and taken me to a place called "prosperous."

> As with all things with God, He lays out principles in His Word, and His ways work!

Why Wasn't My Giving Working?

You see, there was a time that I lived in a house so small that you could do everything you needed to do in the bathroom without moving a step in any direction. There was a time that my wife scraped pennies together to walk to the store to buy macaroni and cheese for us to eat. There was a time that I suffered serious lack…and I was a good Christian and a giver!

So what was wrong? Why wasn't my giving working? Simple: I was ignorant to what the WORD said and ignorant to the importance of PURPOSE. So, although I had a good heart, the devil robbed me blind...but no more! I didn't know how to use my true motive to do what I wanted to do. I had a "throw" instead of "sow" mentality that was lacking purpose. As with all things with God, He lays out principles in His Word, and His ways work! So, here are a few principles that I've learned that helped me. I hope they will help you, too.

God Will Only Do What He Said He Will Do

The four main ways of giving mentioned in the Bible are these:

- **The Tithe**—people struggle with it.
- **Firstfruits**—people don't believe in it.
- **Alms**—people totally understand it.
- **Seed**—people think it's a gamble.

God wants us to do all of these, but He offers *different* results for each of the four types of giving. That means that not all giving is the same. You see, you can *only* expect God to do what He *says*...and believe me, what He says is enough! Whether it's spiritual, physical, financial or otherwise, you can have faith in the Word and yet misapply its teachings and not reap the results you were expecting. Of these four types of giving, three are towards God and one is towards man.

Purpose is key. Whatever you PURPOSE in your heart, that's what you give—not grudgingly nor of NECESSITY (meaning you should not be moved by need), because God loves a CHEERFUL giver (2 Corinthians 9:7). Never forget that God meant what He wrote in the Word and if we want to succeed in this life—no matter whether it's spiritual, physical, financial, or otherwise—then we must live by His ways. So, if we want to excel in life, we've got to learn those ways and apply them. This is true in every respect, including the way we give.

Many times, Christians will say that giving in any specific way is an "Old Testament" principle and that all of it has been done away with because we have been saved by grace and are "New Testament" believers. But Christ Himself warned us that He did not come to do away with everything that came before Him, but to fulfill the purity of God's law down to the last "jot" and "tittle" until "Heaven and Earth pass away" (Matthew 5:18). I find that believers who say the Old Testament is irrelevant to us today usually just want to get out of giving the tithe, because in all my years of ministry, I've never heard them bring up the argument regarding anything else!

> God wants us to do all of these, but He offers different results for each of the four types of giving.

When I want to show why I believe tithing is relevant for New Testament believers, I bring up Melchisedec, a King-Priest of Jerusalem in the Old Testament who "blessed" Abraham. In return, Abraham gave him 10% of what he'd gathered in battle (Genesis 14). Melchisedec is referred to in the Bible as a type of Christ and, in fact, in the book of Hebrews, Jesus Christ is repeatedly referred to as *"Called of God an high priest after the order of Melchisedec"* (Hebrews 5:10).

So, now that we've established it as biblical, let's break down these four types of giving.

Chapter Two

The Tithe

"The blessing" was given to us before "the tithe." The famous tithe scripture found in Malachi chapter 3 shows us how our giving to God works to put us back under "the blessing" that was originally bestowed on mankind.

The Word says, *"Will a man rob God? Yet ye have robbed Me. But ye say, Wherein have we robbed Thee? In tithes and offerings. Ye are cursed with a curse: for ye have robbed Me, even this whole nation. Bring ye all the tithes into the storehouse, that there may be meat in Mine house, and prove Me now herewith, saith the LORD of hosts, if I will not open you the windows of heaven, and pour you out a blessing, that there shall not be room enough to receive it. And I will rebuke the devourer for your*

> Malachi chapter 3 shows us how our giving to God works to put us back under "the blessing" that was originally bestowed on mankind.

sakes, and he shall not destroy the fruits of your ground; neither shall your vine cast her fruit before the time in the field, saith the LORD of hosts. And all nations shall call you blessed: for ye shall be a delightsome land, saith the LORD of hosts" (Malachi 3:8-12).

"The blessing" was given to man at the very beginning. What was it? It was God's hand on their lives. Then He gave *direction* to mankind on how to operate within the world He had created for them. Genesis 1:27-28 says, *"So God created man in His own image, in the image of God created He him; male and female created He them. And **God blessed them**, and God said unto them, **Be fruitful**, and **multiply**, and **replenish** the earth, and **subdue** it: and have dominion over the fish of the sea, and over the fowl of the air, and over every living thing that moveth upon the earth."*

> Tithing is the way for recessions and depressions to bypass you.

Notice that God's very first *words* of wisdom to mankind about how to operate under His wonderful hand of blessing are commanded right after the blessing is given.

God said, *be fruitful*—which means always producing.
God said, *multiply*—which means always increasing.
God said, *replenish*—which means fill and re-fill.
God said, *subdue*—which means control your environment or your environment will control you.

So, Genesis reveals that "the blessing" is ours when we are in a state of obedience to God's commands—as Adam and Eve were before they disobeyed God. And Malachi reveals that "the blessing" is also connected to the tithe—in other words, what we lost in the beginning through disobedience, we regain through obedience. Obviously, God cares about giving and honor because they reveal the condition of the heart.

So, in "the blessing" and in the commands given afterwards, God gave us answers before we ever asked questions. He gave us trees before He ever asked for seed. And those four things He told us to do—be fruitful, multiply, replenish, and subdue—are all *conditions* that go along with being blessed as we operate in life. They are actions that we must take in order to succeed and they apply to all areas of life.

Again, the "tithe," which is *God's portion*, is the divine connector to "the blessing," which is *our portion* (Genesis 1:28, *"Be fruitful..."*). I want to establish that before I go further.

The Motivation is OBEDIENCE

The motivation for tithing must be obedience, which is a sign that you have faith not only in God as your Father, but also in God as your Supplier and the Protector of what belongs to you. Tithing is the way for recessions and depressions to bypass you. As long as the windows of Heaven are open to you, the Word says that applying the principle of the tithe in faith will insulate you from the recessions and depressions or the tumultuousness of world economics.

Tithing holds God to His promise to open the windows

of Heaven and rebuke the devourer. What is "the devourer"? It's anything that comes up in life that makes you spend money you don't want to spend. It's unexpected financial hits like your cars or appliances breaking down early or poor yields when you should have more. It's things falling through the cracks.

We use the Scripture to understand God's way of doing things. He asks for the tithe so there will be "meat" in His house, which is the church. So, in God's mind, the tithe belongs to the church. It keeps it not only operating, but also flourishing so that it continues to be an outreach to the community and the world at large.

The church is a priceless asset to society. It is a place not only to learn *about* God, but also to find God as Savior and Lord, and to be healed of our wounds as we unify with other human beings. The church is a place to gather and worship with others of like precious faith.

> Remember that God is never thinking of Himself when He asks us to do something.

The church is a safe haven where the Word is taught and demonstrated. The reason it's so valuable to society is because only God can change the heart of a man or a woman. There must be a place for us to congregate and find strength in unity and share the teachings God gave us with the world.

You see, it takes a heart-change to see a true life-change. Once Christ is received as Savior (and that can happen anywhere), the church helps to facilitate the growth of people so that they can learn God's ways and become what God created them to be. Society needs God because people need God, and people need each other—society is a better place when its people are better people! The tithe brings "meat" into His house and it's a very important command from God.

Remember that God is never thinking of Himself when He asks us to do something. He has everything He needs! Ultimately, He is thinking about *us*. So, when He says, *"Bring ye all the tithes into the storehouse, that there may be meat in Mine house..."* (Malachi 3:10), He is actually not trying to get something *from* us; He is trying to get something *to* us.

What is He trying to get to us? The blessing of living under an open-windowed Heaven and protection! Read it with me now: *"...and prove Me now herewith, saith the LORD of hosts, if I will not open you the windows of Heaven, and pour you out a blessing, that there shall not be room enough to receive it. And I will rebuke the devourer for your sakes, and he shall not destroy the fruits of your ground; neither shall your vine cast her fruit before the time in the field, saith the LORD of hosts. And all nations shall call you blessed: for ye shall be a delightsome land, saith the LORD of hosts"* (Malachi 3:10-12).

We tap into the "Power Source" when we go beyond just reading those verses and start applying them and actually pull down the promises with our faith. Tithing is supposed to be purposeful. In other words, it's not just something you throw into the church bucket without thinking; it is a tangible way you are obeying your Father.

Nothing works without faith. So if you want tithing to "work" for you, then have faith in God. Just like you would pray for healing or the salvation of a loved one, consider what you are doing with your tithe. Quote scripture when you pray for those open windows of Heaven and thank God for rebuking of the devourer. Use the scripture in your prayers and watch God work!

Remember, the tithe is something the Word says God requires for you to be connected to "the blessing." It's 10%. If ever you feel like it's too much, remember that it's better to be 90% blessed than 100% cursed! But don't let the "curse" part scare you. All you have to do to get out from under the curse and instead put yourself under the blessing is to start obeying God. He knows your situation personally and sees your heart, but He requires obedience and faith in order to get what He promised. Remember, you can't change what you didn't do in the past, but you *can* change your future.

> God wants you to hold Him to His promise to rebuke "the devourer" on your behalf!

The "blessed" life is for you! Speak it over your own life. In fact, I suggest you pray those verses each time you tithe to remind yourself and God of His promise. Don't feel bad about praying to God about your tithe. God *wants* you to hold Him to His promise to rebuke "the devourer" on your behalf! That's why He says, *"prove Me!"* That means He wants you to *think* about what you are doing. So, don't dismiss Him. Give God what He is due, and don't just tithe without thinking. Instead, pull on God's promise with your faith and the words of your mouth.

The Tithe is for Everyone: Laymen, Clergy, Churches, and Organizations of All Kinds

Also, it's interesting to note that God was talking to the preachers when He talked about being robbed. Why? Because the principle of giving back the tithe was a command to everyone, but it was often taught by clergy who didn't practice it. Obviously, God wasn't too happy about that. His principle of "giving back" applies to every believer and the organizations they run—that means laymen, clergy, churches, ministries, businesses, humanitarian organizations, etc. It's an across-the-board command to the believer and we should ALL do it in obedience to God.

That's why, even though this ministry is a church, we GIVE all four ways.

Cathy and I give personally, of course, but we also make sure that this organization that has been put under our care is also giving the tithe, as well as giving in the other ways God's Word has taught us. Why? Because I don't want this ministry to live under a closed Heaven! I want to honor God with the tithe, firstfruits, alms, and seed! I believe that my heart and my purposeful giving is what has kept both this ministry and me personally out of deficit all these many years.

Imagine how much we could do if every person and every organization tithed!

Chapter Three

Firstfruits

The concept of firstfruits was very important to the Jews, who were an agricultural society. They would bring the first part of their harvest as a special offering to God during the celebration of Pentecost. It was a way of honoring God out of their new abundance. The motivation was nothing more than generosity…and God took notice! The heart is very important to God when it comes to all giving.

There are 31 references to the principle of giving God the "firstfruits" in the Bible, and the verses are found in both Old and New Testaments (referring to offerings of ourselves, both physical and spiritual), but the passage about firstfruits that I want to look at today is the most straightforward when it comes to the promise of God regarding this type of giving. It tells you what you should do and what God promises to do in return.

It's found in Proverbs 3:9-10: *"Honour the LORD with thy substance, and with the firstfruits of all thine increase: So shall thy barns be filled with plenty, and thy presses shall burst out with new wine."*

God says that if you "honor" Him with the "firstfruits" of your "INCREASE," then your "barns" (which literally means storing place) will be filled with "plenty" and your "presses" (which literally means trough or vat) will "burst" with new wine. So, these verses are about how you handle the increase of your substance. In other words, what do you do when you get blessed? For those in the Bible who were mostly dealing with animals and agriculture, the firstfruits offering was tied to the time when the crops yield their increase.

The Motivation is GENEROSITY

What is "firstfruits" in today's world? Some believe the firstfruits of your "increase" begins with a calendar year, as in the offering you give at the first of the year—the principle being that you honor God first and, since it is the beginning of a New Year, what better time to show Him generosity? It's a great principle. However, I believe the firstfruits extends beyond that because this type of giving is directly connected to your "increase"—and that could come at any moment and on any day during the calendar year.

> The firstfruits offering is an expression of your love and, again, it is only done ONCE.

So, how do I define a firstfruits offering? It's what you give to God when you come into what I like to call an "extra blessing"—and it should be the "first" of ANY increase bestowed upon you that will be ongoing in your life. This very specific type of giving is an offering ONLY GIVEN ONCE on your

INCREASE, not your INCOME, and it should be given FIRST as a form of honor to God.

The best modern day example I can give you for this is if you get a raise in your income at your place of employment—this would be an **actual increase** in finances that you didn't have before and will be an ongoing increase in your life. The "firstfruits" would be the first time you see the increase and it is an offering you only give ONCE. In other words, the first paycheck that you see the increase on, that amount of increase would be given as a special "firstfruits" offering to God.

Why does God *want* you to give firstfruits?

Firstfruits shows God you're not in love with money; that's why He trusts you with it. Again, let your motive be generosity—an offering that shows you are thankful to God for blessing you and you want to give out of the generosity of your heart. This offering shows your gratitude to God for the extra blessing He has bestowed upon you. The firstfruits offering is an expression of your love and, again, it is only done ONCE.

The firstfruits offering is considered holy. It bridges both Testaments and, as believers, this concept is often used to link us to Christ. Romans 11:16 says, *"For if the firstfruit be holy, the lump is also holy: and if the root be holy, so are the branches."*

So, the concept of giving firstfruits as a *tangible* offering is honorable and holy to God. The reward for doing so is storage places filled with plenty and troughs and vats filled with something fresh and new and bursting out. Likewise, the concept of *spiritual* firstfruits is also honorable and holy to God. Jesus Christ gave Himself as a firstfruits offering and we are also the firstfruits of His new creation. He is the vine, and He is holy. Therefore, as His branches, we too are made holy in the sight of God.

The firstfruits offering is important to God in every respect. More than most types of giving, the firstfruits offering is truly heart-driven and given as a direct form of gratitude to God.

You Have to do Things God's Way

Believing changes *everything*, but when it comes to giving, *purpose* and *obedience* are what I've found matter the most. If you want to do the most you can for God and mankind—and you want to see God's blessings on your life as a result—then you have to do things God's way.

As I mentioned earlier, there was a time in my life that I suffered serious lack, even though I was a good Christian and a giver. Why wasn't my giving working? How was it that I could give with a good heart and still not see the results I wanted? Well, the truth is that I was ignorant to what the WORD said about what I was actually doing.

I had a good heart and did the best I knew to do but, back then, I didn't prosper very much. Why? Because I didn't give the way God said to! Today, things are a lot different. As I said, I don't have to tell you that I'm a blessed man. I haven't had a financial deficit in my 35 years of ministry and I'm living proof that *anyone* can use God's Word to "Believe the Unbelievable and Receive the Impossible"—whether it's spiritual, physical, financial, or otherwise.

You see, God's Word works, but He is under no

obligation to do something He never said He'd do. That's why it's a good idea to understand more about His ways when it comes to giving.

I've found that if you want to bless others and also be blessed, it's critical that you understand these ways—that you understand what the Word says and apply it. When I personally began to understand what the scriptures said about giving, it changed the way I not only thought, but also believed. And, as I said, believing changes everything!

Today, I sow with *purpose*. I understand the incredible power of *obedience*. I am also very interested in the *motive* behind giving. And I know without a shadow of doubt that God WILL do what He said…no more and no less! So, because I have gained some knowledge and wisdom, I can put my faith on the Word with confidence—and I have seen *results* I once never would have dreamed of. I'm a blessed man and not just financially, but in every sense of the word.

God wants you to be blessed. I believe that as you honor God by obeying His Word and giving with purpose, you will see these kinds of results, too. And the first step towards the blessed life is learning and following His way of doing things.

> Today, I sow with purpose. I understand the incredible power of obedience. I am also very interested in the motive behind giving.

Now, I want to focus on giving alms because I believe it is the way people around the world give the most.

Chapter Four

Alms

I'd say that 95% of all giving is alms giving—and it makes sense because this type of giving is one that everyone understands, because it deals directly with something we can see with our own eyes in the world around us: lack!

Alms is a gift given to the poor and to those in desperate need. Throughout the Bible, you will find story after story of the Lord's people giving to the poor. Why? Because we have ALL been made in the image of God and so, whether we are a sinner or a believer, there is an element of compassion in all human beings.

The Motivation is COMPASSION

Job helped the poor out of his abundance—and said that if he didn't do it, he may as well have his arms fall off and his bones be broken. Tabitha helped the poor and did many good deeds—and the Word says Peter came and prayed for her after she died and she was raised up from the dead. Cornelius helped the poor—and the Lord came to Him in a vision and said that his prayers and alms giving had literally become a "memorial to God." And, of course, Jesus helped the poor—so much so that when He sent Judas away at the Lord's Supper, because He knew he'd betrayed Him, everyone in the room assumed that Jesus had sent Judas to give alms to the poor. So, we know without a shadow of doubt that it is the Christian duty to help those in need and we know it is also a joy to be able to help others.

The story of the Good Samaritan resonates because we see someone who is literally robbed, beaten, and stripped of all his belongings. Now, we aren't told what the economic status of this man is *before* he is robbed, but I have to say that thieves generally don't rob and strip a poor man! Yet, this man *becomes* poor through the misdeeds of others. Through this parable, Christ tells us that we are not to dismiss these cases or even just pray about them, but we are to physically do something to help. And we know that it's not only believers who strive to help the poor, whether they start out in poverty or become impoverished by the evil deeds of men. The scripture tells us that even Zacchaeus, who was a known sinner, was a great alms giver. So, we all understand alms giving.

God's Rate of Exchange

What we *don't* all understand, however, is what God promises us in return when we help the poor. You see, all God's ways of sowing and reaping have a rate of exchange explained in His Word, and are conditional upon the type of giving.

Notice that with the tithe, God's promise is that He will

"open the windows of Heaven" and *"rebuke the devourer."* In other words, you gain access to His blessing and He helps you with things that fall through the cracks.

Notice that with firstfruits, God promises that because you honor Him in this way, *"your barns will be filled with plenty and your presses will burst out with new wine."* In other words, your storage places have plenty and He can trust you with money.

When it comes to alms giving, which is probably the way that the majority of the world gives, God again is very specific about what He promises in return. What is the rate of return on giving alms to the poor? It is one thing and one thing alone: REPAYMENT.

> What we don't all understand, however, is what God promises us in return when we help the poor.

God says if you will pity the poor and give alms, He considers it a loan to Him and He promises that He will REPAY you. In other words, it's a dollar-for-dollar reimbursement. Proverbs 19:17 makes His promise very plain: *"He that hath pity upon the poor lendeth unto the LORD; and that which he hath given will He pay him again."*

This is the biggest reason why people will say that their "giving isn't working"—because they sow seeds one way and expect to reap a way other than what God promised. You can't plant corn and expect an apple tree. God is bound by His Word and He only has to do what He promises to do. There is no open-windowed Heaven with alms giving. There is no rebuking of the devourer. There are no barns of plenty or any bursting out of new wine. There is no 30, 60, or 100-fold return. The promise God made to us is repayment for the loan.

Alms giving should be a part of your life of giving. We should ALL give to the poor and lend to the Lord, but we should also be aware that the rate of return is what God promised—repayment—and we can't blame God for not blessing us with something He never promised to do. This is why I don't like to mix up my giving. I like to give with *purpose* so that I know what I'm doing when I'm doing it and can use my faith for what God promised.

Some people don't care. They don't want anything back. But I'm not one of those people—I consider it kind of selfish to be honest. Why do I care about the rate of exchange? Because I'm a sower and not a thrower! And I know one very practical truth, and it is this: The best thing I can do for a poor person is *not* to be poor!

> This is the biggest reason why people will say that their "giving isn't working"—because they sow seeds one way and expect to reap a way other than what God promised.

The more I reap, the more I have to give to the poor—it's as simple as that. I want to give *more* to the poor. I want to lend the Lord *more* this year than I did last year. I want to help people. My heart and the Scripture compel me to give alms.

But I also know that if alms giving is my *only* giving,

then the hard truth is that I'm not going to have the yield I want in order to grow financially. In fact, the repayment God promised me means that I will end up exactly where I started from financially. And it's sad to say, but if all I do is give alms and I dismiss being a tither, well…even that repayment could be devoured as it's on its way back to me! So, I'm well aware of the importance of alms giving, but by no means is it the *only* way I give. To do so would be direct disobedience, in my opinion, because God has given us His Word, which says otherwise. Yet I see so many people who do just this and claim their giving isn't working! Guess what? It IS working…and it's working exactly the way God said it would.

The Importance of Human Dignity—Most People Directly Disobey Jesus in Alms Giving

Over the years, my Board of Directors has often told me that I should talk more about my alms giving and what the ministry does to help those in need. But there is something in my heart that will not allow me to parade these people around just because I helped them.

You see, God loves people with a love you probably can't fathom—and do you realize that He is concerned about their well-being in a way that sometimes smacks right up against our natural tendencies? Jesus Christ was very specific about the METHOD of giving to the poor. And yet He also revealed a cruel and very real fact of life: the poor we will have with us ALWAYS (Mark 14:7).

So, according to Jesus, no amount of alms giving will

ever eradicate poverty, and yet this is the type of giving that the entire world understands and does the most. God Himself tells us that alms literally have the weakest yield in terms of reaping. Perhaps it is because this is the only type out of the four I'm teaching about that is not given to God, but directly given to mankind.

Why will we have the poor with us always, as Christ said? I believe it is because you can't solve a long-term poverty problem with a short-term alms offering—the human race, while compassionate at heart, is also evil at heart. Man's inhumanity to man not only *facilitates* poverty, but often, actually, *promotes* it. And there are times when the very act of giving alms in a *disobedient* way steals the very thing that God wants poor people to hang onto: **dignity!**

I find it very disturbing that most giving to the poor is done in a way that is in **direct disobedience to what Jesus Christ said to do**. Just look at what Jesus has to say about it in Matthew 6:1-4: *"Take heed that ye do not your alms before men, to be seen of them: otherwise ye have no reward of your Father which is in Heaven.* ***Therefore when thou doest thine alms, do not sound a trumpet before thee****, as the hypocrites do in the synagogues and in the streets, that they may have glory of men. Verily I say unto you, They have their reward. But **when thou doest alms, let not thy left hand know what thy right hand doeth: That thine alms may be in secret***: and thy Father which seeth in secret Himself **shall reward thee openly**.*"

Tabitha was rewarded openly, Cornelius was rewarded openly, Job was rewarded openly, and so were the others who were recorded in Scripture for their giving and for what happened to them as a result of God seeing what they did—and that's about as "openly" as you can get!

So, why doesn't Jesus want us to talk about this type of giving? And notice that this is the ONLY type of giving that the Word commands us *not* to talk about. God is not opposed to you talking about your tithe, your firstfruits or your seed giving, but He is VERY MUCH opposed to you talking about your alms giving.

> I find it very disturbing that most giving to the poor is done in a way that is in direct disobedience to what Jesus Christ said to do.

Why? Because this is something that Christ calls "secret" giving—and He wants it to be a secret to such a degree that He says that if you actually promote yourself for doing it or do it outside of *secrecy*, you lose ALL your rights to a divine reward. Your reward becomes the opinions of others and that's it! So, why does Jesus tell us this?

Alms are given in secrecy to protect people's dignity in their crisis. God doesn't want you to talk about or tell anyone about your alms giving—anything you do to help a poor person—for that reason. God does NOT want them being made a spectacle in their time of need. God does not want them to be put in a position that lowers them in any way whatsoever—not in your eyes, not in other people's eyes, and especially not in their own eyes. I cannot say this enough!

Love Gives, But it Gives the RIGHT Way

Our job as believers and fellow human beings is to love one another—and you do not show love for a person who is in crisis by parading the fact that you helped them, or by telling others about what you did for them in an effort to show your good deed. God sees. Let that be enough, knowing and believing in faith that GOD will openly reward you for whatever you do for the poor.

Love gives—it doesn't ignore a poor person. Love also respects—it doesn't show off at the expense of the one you helped. In fact, look what happens when you apply the God-kind of love that is explained in 1 Corinthians 13:4-8 to the poor: You'll suddenly see how easily doing a good deed can become something that actually can harm a human being on a greater level than tangible needs.

Love is kind—in the same way kindness compels you to give alms to a person in poverty, kindness should also compel you to keep your mouth shut so that you don't lower that person's self-esteem further. Kindness does anything it can in order not to make the receiver of charity feel small. The only way to avoid this is to "not let your right hand know what your left hand is doing." In other words, give in secrecy and let it go. Just

> **God is not opposed to you talking about your tithe, your firstfruits, or your seed giving, but He is VERY MUCH opposed to you talking about your alms giving.**

as you don't tell others, don't remind the poor person what you did for them. If you do, I've got two words for you: REWARD LOST!

Love doesn't envy or parade itself—never give alms in an effort to gain self-importance over another person you think is a bigger giver of alms than you. It sounds crazy, but there are people who actually fall into this trap of one-upmanship. Usually they are preachers or humanitarian leaders, but it happens with others, too. If you do this to gain prominence in the community or over another giver, guess what? Reward lost!

Love isn't puffed up—giving alms out of a "look at me" mindset is wrong. That's a good deed masked in pride. Reward lost! Love doesn't behave rudely—when you give, don't make the poor feel like they are a burden or a hassle. That's rude and it's not God's way.

Love doesn't seek its own when it comes to poverty—there is no situation in the world where you should take advantage of someone when they have hit a rough spot. God calls us to help the poor and not to use their poverty as an excuse to exercise control over them. This is so plain wrong it should go without saying, but many people have capitalized on the weakened financial state of the poor. God sees this! In the same way He sees secret alms giving and rewards openly, I believe He sees when the poor are taken advantage of, and those who do it will reap the consequences openly.

Love is not provoked and love doesn't think evil of the poor—don't allow yourself to fall into the trap of griping about how the poor person got to the crisis point. Even if it appears as if it's their own fault, don't make that judgment call!

You may think you know the situation but, in all likelihood, you don't have the full picture like God does.

Think about the parable of the Good Samaritan again: I'm sure there were people who saw the poor man and thought maybe he wouldn't have gotten to that state if he'd done something different. Thank God we serve a Father Who has the power to deliver us from our own destruction if we call upon His name. But if we see someone who has fallen into crisis, we should be compelled by love to help them up…whether we think they "deserve" it or not! Again, it's not our place to judge. That's God's job. Our place is to love.

Love does not rejoice in iniquity but rejoices in truth—I don't care how bad someone was, if you rejoice in the sin that got them there and say, "You see! That's what you get!" then you are not acting in love, even if you give them a little alms. Think about the prodigal son: His poverty came at his own hand, and yet love took him and helped him anyway.

> Just as you don't tell others, don't remind the poor person what you did for them. If you do, I've got two words for you: REWARD LOST.

Remember that love rejoices in the truth—and the only real truth is Jesus Christ and Him crucified, and the teachings God gave us, which not only set us free personally, but also help us to set others free, too. Love is a powerful attribute that bears all things, believes all things, hopes all things, and endures all things—simply put, love never fails.

I think that one of the best things you can do is to believe in somebody. Encourage them! Give them hope! The truth that set you free isn't just something you talk about; it should be something you *do*. This is the Christlike life. And we do the poor an advantage by not only giving in secret, but also by treating them with respect.

I believe that there is a reason why some poor people bristle at taking charity; why they will sometimes even resent the person who helped them. Sometimes their anger is their misguided way of trying to regain the personal dignity they feel they've lost. They want to do it themselves, and that's a good thing! You see, as human beings, we want in our hearts to be equal with one another and, from the time of the Garden of Eden, God created us to work. Notice that God gave Adam a job before He even gave him a wife!

Yet, I also believe this is why some poor people are "takers" and will allow others to pour out alms all day long and never lift a finger to succeed in life—because they honestly believe in their heart that they ARE less capable than the one doing the giving. So, they end up feeling like, since they are lower on the totem pole, they are *entitled* to the help.

In other words, somewhere along the way, these types of people got the wrong idea about who they are… somewhere along the way, they lost their dignity! It could have been lost in childhood, it could have been lost by how they were raised to think, it could have been lost through disappointment, or lost through the cruel hand of others. But somewhere along the way, they lost who they are as human beings…they lost their dignity.

As Christians and alms givers, we shouldn't make that

loss of dignity worse by giving to them openly and patting ourselves on the back as we do it. Alms should always and forever be secret giving. Otherwise, not only do we lose our reward from God, but we also further keep the poor feeling down in life. This should not be! Obey the words of Jesus and consider your ways.

Not All Giving is the Same

As we've been learning, God offers *different* results for different types of giving in His Word. I believe that if He offers different results for different types of giving, then all giving is NOT the same. We serve an orderly God. And we can *only* expect God to do what He *says* He will do—nothing more; nothing less.

In this book, I have shared the results you can expect when giving the **tithe** *(people struggle with it)*, the **firstfruits** *(people don't believe in it)* and **alms** *(people totally understand it)*. And now, I want to deal with my favorite of these four ways of giving: **seed**. When it comes to seed, *people think it's a gamble*. But the truth is that there is no "Gospel casino" in the Word.

Heaven and Earth may pass away, but God's Word will not. Sowing and reaping will one day not be needed...but today, while the earth still remains, this principle remains (Genesis 8:22). Now, let's learn some things about it.

Chapter Five

Seed

When I learned about seed sowing and began to apply the scriptural principle concerning seed, it literally changed everything in the financial aspect of my personal life and in the way my ministry both gave and received.

As I mentioned in the beginning of this book, the first message in which I dealt with seed on an entirely higher level was, "Hey! That's My Harvest!" That message was birthed out of a revelation God showed me about a personal seed I had sown years before. That revelation changed the way I thought about giving, and from then until now, I have been on a journey of understanding more and more about God's amazing system of sowing seed and reaping harvests.

SEED: The motivation is faith and reward. It is the only way that the 30, 60, and 100-fold harvest can be received.

So, what is seed? It is "offering" giving, which means that seed sowing begins at **11%** because the tithe (which means a tenth - 10%) belongs to the Lord. This means that you can't expect God to bless you again, or rebuke the devourer again, or open windows He's already opened when you sow *seed*. Why? Because that's only what He's promised in His Word when you give your *tithe*.

And you can't expect your barns or storage places to be filled with plenty again when you sow *seed* because that's only what He's promised in His Word with your *firstfruits* giving.

And you also can't expect God to "repay" you when you sow *seed* because that's only what He's promised to do in His Word with your *alms* giving.

Seed sowing is different because it literally has numbers attached to it as a promise in the Word. This means that when you give a seed offering, you have something you can attach your faith to that is very concrete in nature.

What does God promise concerning seed sowing? He promises that if you sow into good ground, you will reap 30, 60 or 100-fold of whatever it is that you sowed. When it comes to financial seed sowing, God of course leaves the amount you sow up to you, but He retains the right to multiply it back in one of three ways: 30, 60 or 100-fold. I like to say that you pick the denomination and He picks the multiplication.

Is the Moon Made of Cheese? What Defines "the Word" to You?

Most people don't believe in seed sowing like this any more than they believe the moon is made of cheese! But I don't care who says what to discredit it, this type of giving is biblical, it works, and its text is found in "The Parable of the Sower."

Let's look at what Jesus shared and see how this parable and its explanation apply to financial seed sowing. *"Hearken; Behold, there went out a sower to sow: And it came to pass, as he sowed, some fell by the way side, and the fowls of the air came and devoured it up. And some fell on stony ground, where it had not much earth; and immediately it sprang up, because it had no depth of earth: But when the sun was up, it was scorched; and because it had no root, it withered away. And some fell among thorns, and the thorns grew up, and choked it, and it yielded no fruit. **And other fell on good ground, and did yield fruit that sprang up and increased; and brought forth, some thirty, and some sixty, and some an hundred**. And he said unto them, He that hath ears to hear, let him hear"* (Mark 4:3-9).

> He promises that if you sow into good ground, you will reap 30, 60 or 100-fold of whatever it is that you sowed.

The disciples of Jesus didn't understand the parable and they asked Him to explain it. But before He did, He asked them a couple of point-blank questions: *"Know ye not this parable? And how then will ye know all parables?"* (Mark 4:13). In other words, if you don't understand this one, you won't understand any of the rest! That's the first clue that sowing and reaping is relative to everything in life.

Jesus then proceeds to explain it further: *"The sower soweth the Word. And these are they by the way side, where the Word is sown; but when they have heard, Satan cometh immediately, and taketh away the Word that was sown in their hearts. And these are they likewise which are sown on stony ground; who, when they have heard the Word, immediately receive it with gladness; And have no root in themselves, and so endure but for a time: afterward, when affliction or persecution ariseth for the Word's sake, immediately they are offended. And these are they which are sown among thorns; such as hear the Word, And the cares of this world, and the deceitfulness of riches, and the lusts of other things entering in, choke the Word, and it becometh unfruitful. And these are they which are sown on good ground; such as hear the Word, and receive it, and bring forth fruit, some thirtyfold, some sixty, and some an hundred"* (Mark 4:14-20).

> **The seed offering is anything above and beyond the tithe—it is not alms or firstfruits giving.**

So, what does "the Word" mean to you? Because this is exactly what "the sower" is sowing in Christ's explanation of this famous parable. Is "the Word" wisdom about how to live life? Is it prophecy? Is it only the story of Jesus Christ's birth, death, and resurrection? Does "the Word" *only* contain information about how to be saved? It can't be because Jesus shared this before He went to the cross…so, again, what does "the Word" mean to you?

If you believe that "the Word" is defined only by verses that lead people to salvation, then you have a lot fewer pages in your Bible than I do. Salvation IS the most important thing, but it is not the ONLY thing in the Word.

If that were true, then we might as well die upon accepting Jesus as Lord and go on to Heaven. But we were created to LIVE, and salvation opens up the door so that we can live as we ought to live…and I believe that is by living *"in Earth, as it is in Heaven"* as Jesus prayed in "The Lord's Prayer" (Matthew 6:10). What is it like in Heaven? Is anybody broke there? Do they have issues with love or generosity…or lack? Let the elevator go to the top!

I believe that "the Word" is what it says it is—the Bible—and any of its concepts that you open your heart up to and "sow" into your heart will reproduce, but it will only reproduce after its own kind. Galatians 6:7-8 is so plain: *"Be not deceived; God is not mocked: for whatsoever a man soweth, that shall he also reap."* So, what does "whatsoever" mean? Let me help you: it means *whatsoever!* Do finances fall into that category? Yes, they do…and so does everything else! That's why Jesus said that if you don't get this parable, then you won't get any of them.

Are finances in the Bible? What if the "whatsoever" you choose to sow IS a financial offering—what will you reap in return for the seed you sow? I'll tell you: a financial harvest! Why? Because *whatsoever* a man sows, that, and only that, will he also reap. And the multiplication rate on what you sow will be *exactly* as Jesus said it would be, which is 30, 60 or 100-fold.

"Fertile" Ground Just Makes Sense

The seed offering is anything above and beyond the tithe—it is not alms or firstfruits giving. It is an offering you give specifically as seed sown, expecting a harvest of 30, 60 or 100-fold. And that seed must be *sown* (meaning *given*) into a work of the Lord that is fertile, which means it's reproducing and growing the body of Christ.

Your seed must be sown into fertile soil if it is to accomplish the impossible in life—and the 30, 60 and 100-fold return is an "unbelievable" and "impossible" thing. It's mind-boggling! This type of giving, based on the cornerstone parable of Christ, works. But if your giving is not "seed" and the soil you choose is not producing and increasing—as fertile soil does—there will be little to no harvest.

Sometimes people give all their offerings to organizations that are not producing—they are only taking and maintaining. That's not fertile. Fertile soil is a place that is *increasing* in doing something good—it's a growing place.

Fertile soil is NOT a church that is always busted and broke, or a ministry that is always going under. It's also not a humanitarian organization that uses more for its operating expenses than it uses to serve its original purpose. No, the best yield is seed sown into fertile soil—a place that is GROWING and DOING what it has set out to do. Sowing into fertile soil just makes sense.

The Wonder of Faith and Reward

What is the critical element in seed sowing? It's the same element that is in every other type of giving: PURPOSE. If you don't know where you're going, you're not going to know when you get there. If you don't know how you're giving, you're not going to know what you're receiving in return. And reaping IS important, because the more you grow yourself and give with purpose, the more you will do for God and humanity.

Seed sowing and harvesting on my giving brought me to a higher place in life. When I grasped the concept and put my faith toward it, it began to bring back harvests to me that changed my financial circumstances. As I've said, I have spoken a lot on the power of seed because I started to see how the principle could help so many people. The more I gave and told others about what I'd learned, the more I saw the cycle of blessings in my life and in the lives of those I told.

Now, I know some people don't believe this, but I do! This was something I could put my faith towards. It was so specific that I could tell if the devil was trying to steal it. I would "call it in" with the words of my mouth daily—and I would notice when my harvests came in. I wasn't giving haphazardly anymore. Best of all, I could honor God in greater and greater ways, both with my testimony and with my increased financial blessings. And as a result, I had more to give in the form of the tithe, firstfruits, alms and, of course, seed.

> What is the critical element in seed sowing? It's the same element that is in every other type of giving: PURPOSE.

You see, God reacts to this level of faith with great rewards—notice how specific He is about it. He attached those numbers for a reason. As Einstein famously said,

"God doesn't play dice." Jesus didn't just throw those "30, 60 and 100-fold" words out there just to kill time as He told the parable! Oh, no, He said it with PURPOSE, just like He said and did everything else.

The seed concept changes everything. As for me, I already believed that it applied to spiritual areas, as well as to how I treated people. As a believer, I already knew that sowing and reaping applied to what I did for others. But before I understood that it also applied to finances, I just wasn't able to do as much as I wanted to do for God, let alone for anybody else. Once I understood it and started giving seed, I saw breakthroughs in my finances that I did not have before—because now my faith was targeted and I refused to let the devil keep me in the dark or steal what rightfully belonged to me.

The Debt Correlation to Seed

I believe that seed sowing is the surest way to stop poverty in your life. I was raised poor. My parents genuinely loved God, but they were mixed up in their giving. Consequently, we never seemed to see much change. You see, haphazard giving brings haphazard results.

I also believe that seed sowing is the quickest way for total debt cancellation to occur. I have heard testimony after testimony from people who have sown seed towards their debts being eliminated, and they've seen it come to pass.

Of course, with purposeful sowing comes a mindset to be more purposeful in other areas. I've spoken about the "fragments" based on the baskets of leftover fish and loaves after Christ's miracle, and I've also encouraged people to remember the verse *"consider your ways,"* too. The story of the fish and loaves in John chapter six shows us that Christ is both a miracle worker and a practical God, and I believe He expects us to follow suit. *"Gather up the fragments that remain that nothing be lost"* applies to finances or "increase" just as much as it applies to everything else.

So many people have told me how sowing seed has changed their finances—how their harvest not only came in the form of direct money, but also in the form of debt cancellation, where what they owed and would've had to pay was suddenly and miraculously removed.

I've seen my own seeds sown in the form of tangible things come back to me in the form of those same types of tangible things. And I can't begin to tell you how many other people have told me their testimony of the same things happening to them, too. God works in mysterious ways, but He always works! The concept of sowing seed, calling it in, recognizing it, and praising God for it by telling others has changed many people's lives and brought them to a place of being more and more blessed financially.

The Devil Can Hinder, But He Can't Stop It—Do Not Faint

I can tell you that sometimes my harvests came in lump sums, while other times they came over time. But the wonderful part about sowing seed with purpose is this: I could always attribute my harvests to the seed sown. I became acutely aware of when I got blessed—I didn't dismiss it ever. No, I took the opportunity to praise God for honoring His Word.

The devil can delay anything—and He has delayed my harvests before—but not forever! Why? Because the Word of God stands and a delay is not a denial. The Word will come to pass if I don't let go of the promise. I refuse to faint.

Galatians 6:9 says, *"And let us not be weary in well doing: for in due season we shall reap, if we faint not."* Weariness will threaten you. So, notice it when it comes, and then simply cast it down. Remember, you aren't actually doing the work, you are calling in the promise.

Don't let seed sowing become burdensome either. I like to make my giving an adventure and a joy. I get excited just considering what God is going to do. But I don't fixate on what I'm getting back so much as I keep moving forward in my life and just keep praying that thing in... with joy! How can I have joy? I can have joy because I don't have fear. Fear brings torment. Faith brings joy! I don't know about you, but I'd rather have joy.

> No farmer goes out the next day and expects to see the seeds he's sown already full grown and producing.

It's a whole lot easier to have childlike faith than it is to have adult-like torment.

So, while I'm in the "growing time" of my seed sowing, I refuse to give up. No farmer goes out the next day and expects to see the seeds he's sown already full grown and producing. Although God does do that sometimes, there is usually time between the seed sown and the harvest reaped. So, during that growing time, I take the opportunity to grow a little myself.

What do I do? I speak the end result. Why? Because I know that my faith is tied to my reward. If I don't believe or if I dismiss what I gave or if I just let it go and not think about it anymore, the devil will do everything he can to stop me and to hold back my blessings. So I remind myself of my seed sown and I "pray it in" so to speak. In other words, I also "sow" the principle of seedtime and harvest into my heart again and again. I don't let go. I consider it "standing"—as in doing all I know to do, I stand therefore (Ephesians 6:13-14). I hold on to the promise. Time will not defeat me, and the bottom line is that faith like this actually does bring the reward of a harvest much quicker.

If you do not believe in the 30, 60 and 100-fold harvest on the seed offerings you sow—and you do not sow those seeds with faith and purpose—you are cutting yourself off from the kind of multiplied blessings that God wants for you. You are not tapping into His way of prosperity. God has so much more for you to receive than you are receiving now. He wants to see you blessed and able to do more.

The Importance of PURPOSE

This is NOT about greed, by no means! The purpose of your giving is important to God and He is not worried about you being blessed like other people are. At some point you have to trust in the God Who trusts in you and realize that following His Word and having faith in Him is what brings you results.

There should be a place for all four types of giving in your life, but you cannot expect the same results on each type. Apples to apples and oranges to oranges—the Word is specific. God sets the rules for the rates of return and nobody can blame Him if they make the mistake of expecting Him to do something He never agreed to do.

This is why I don't mix up my giving. If you take your tithe or your firstfruits or your seed offering and you make it alms, then you just changed the rate of exchange and its purpose. In other words, God will repay you, period! People often take their giving and carve it up into various things and then ask why they aren't getting the results they'd like. I don't do this. I do my best to stick with purposeful giving. I tithe, I give firstfruits, I give alms, and I give seed—and I pray in the promise accordingly.

I don't allow myself to be moved emotionally into giving something I purposed for another area. My tithe remains my tithe—I do not turn it into alms. You see, any giving that you do should NOT be motivated by who "needs" more. That's giving out of "necessity" and God expressly tells us not to give because of need (2 Corinthians 9:7). Why? Because that's emotional giving.

Don't Give Only One Way

If some preacher moves you emotionally to give alms and you choose to give what you originally purposed as the tithe, firstfruits or seed, then you cannot blame God if you don't get the return on your giving that you'd like. Why? Because He set the order.

People often ask me why I give to certain ministries

and churches instead of just giving to those individuals who are in need, and I say this: "Because if I do, I'm going to give the devil access to eat up (devour) whatever blessings I've got, and the window is going to shut down. Besides, giving one way and expecting a result other than what God promised is foolish. It's not what God's Word told me to do."

> People often take their giving and carve it up into various things and then ask why they aren't getting the results they'd like.

If I do not give according to what I know in the Word, then God has no obligation to bless me in the way that I want to be blessed so that I can give MORE. You see, if I gave the way they gave, I'd be in the same boat as they're in: the boat of lack. No thanks!

If I just gave all my tithe, firstfruit, and seed offerings as alms, then I would be playing by my own rules of giving and not God's rules of giving. And while God would repay me, the devil would likely devour most of what I got back and, in the end, I would not be blessed and I would not have more to give. Whew, that's a mouthful! So, I believe it is in the best interest of the Church and the poor that I follow God's ways—because the more blessed I get, the more I get to give—and that's in all *four* areas. You just can't beat God's ways.

A Life of Faith, Peace, and Giving

To me, seed sowing is about being a conduit for blessing all the families of the earth. It's about seeing not only your needs and desires met, but also seeing others find Christ. It's about helping to establish the covenant of God throughout the earth. Alms can't do that. The tithe can't do that. Firstfruits can't do that. But seed? Seed can do that!

Do you notice how the Gospel is spreading around the world so quickly now? The information age has changed everything, but the Church has also begun to understand the power of giving in a whole new way. Some people hate it. They want the Church to go back to being ineffective…to preaching and teaching poverty as they always have. Well, I refuse to do that.

No, I'm one of those many people who have begun to understand what the Word says about giving and how it relates to finances—and how the various ways mentioned all have different results. I believe seed sowing relates to the prosperity of God's people and the furtherance of the Gospel…and I refuse to discount the seedtime and harvest concept just because it makes some people uncomfortable.

Are you kidding me? There is a lost and dying world out there. People need Jesus! And God's people need to be blessed in order to further God's message around the world. This is an economic world. The world doesn't give airtime to Christians for free!

I'm grateful that someone was a Partner to the preacher who led me to the Lord through the medium of television way back in 1974—because if those precious people hadn't given to the work of the Lord, I would not be preaching or writing to you today. But I AM doing just that! Since 1978, I've been spreading His Gospel and the principles I've learned in His Word and I must tell you, it's a great life. It's a life of giving—spiritually, physically, financially, and in every other way—and I love it!

I hope you have learned some things that will help you to live and give with greater purpose in life. Don't worry if you are at the place in life right now where you can't give much. Don't let that thought process keep you down—start today. Trust God and begin to tithe. Then, as increase comes, give a firstfruits offering. Help the poor when you can, no matter whether it is cash or something tangible that they need in life—just be sure that you do it in secret to protect their dignity.

> The tithe—your motive is obedience. Firstfruits—your motive is generosity. Alms—your motive is compassion. Seed—your motive is faith and reward.

And when it comes to seed sowing, don't worry if the seed is small. It does not have to be big for it to work, but your purpose and motivation should be accurate. The tithe—your motive is obedience. Firstfruits—your motive is generosity. Alms—your motive is compassion. Seed—your motive is faith and reward.

The promises of God are for you. *"For all the promises of God in Him are Yes, and in Him Amen, to the glory of God through us. Now He Who establishes us with you in Christ and has anointed us is God, Who also has sealed us and given us the Spirit in our hearts as a guarantee"* (2 Corinthians 1:20-22 NKJV).

Put your faith in the One Who saved you, anointed you, sealed you, and gave you His Spirit in your heart as a guarantee. He is the same God Who is capable of blessing you, of dispelling your fear, and filling you with a deep understanding of His love and His role as Jehovah Jireh, your Provider. If you are willing to walk with Him in the area of your finances and stretch your faith by hearing the Word more and more, you will increase. It all begins with purposeful living.

May this be the time that you have all sufficiency in all things. May it be the time you begin to grow in grace and abound in every good work. May you give to the poor. May God give you seed to sow that you never dreamed possible. May you always have enough to eat and may the God in Heaven that loves you multiply your seed sown… and increase the fruits of your righteousness so that YOU, being enriched in everything, have ALL bountifulness. May you live this kind of 2 Corinthians 8-11 kind of life—one that I believe encompasses all forms of giving and, most importantly, causes you to burst forth with nothing but thanks to the God Who gave it all to you. God bless you as you give and excel in living this *good* life!

Chapter Six

Testimonies

India – My family is very blessed with your ministry. We have learned from you to 'live by our giving.' It works! We are richly blessed by knowing the power of sowing.

Facebook – We have learned SO MUCH from your teachings on what God says about living in a financial society. We have asked God to show us that His Word is true, deciding to simply apply His Word in our lives, and we have seen Him prove Himself over and over again.

Illinois – I have been studying Brother Jesse's teachings on the four types of giving. I have been a Christian for forty years and have never heard about alms and firstfruits. I have always given, but did not understand the principles. I had a large hospital bill. I wrote down the scriptures you gave and said them out loud. I stood on the fact that I am a tither and a giver. The hospital bill of almost $40,000 was canceled.

Indiana – I have yielded to the anointing of wealth! Your DVD changed my life forever. Glory to God! I paid cash for my new house and new car! Thank you for being such a blessing to the world. Keep spreading the Gospel of Jesus Christ to everyone!

Arizona – Thank you for coming to Mesa, Arizona and for sharing your message about the four types of giving. At that time, I was at a very low place—no job for a year, late on three car payments, no home, staying at one friend's house and then the next. Since I heard your message, I've re-launched my business and have gotten caught up on my car payments and am able to support myself. To God be the glory. Your message on the four types of giving was amazing and really stayed with me. Thanks for visiting the church and for really sharing such a powerful message.

Alaska – For many months my husband and I have been studying finances God's way and learning so much! We had gotten ourselves in debt over the years by not being obedient and good stewards. Thankfully we've dug into the Word concerning finances. We've been believing and confessing for a commuter car for my husband and we wanted to save money on gas since he works 45 minutes from home. I felt prompted to sow a seed into your ministry specifically for our car. I obeyed and named it. A few hours later, we were looking online at cars, and I saw one I knew God had arranged just for us. It was even well under our budget and exactly what we needed. Just 24 hours later we had the cash in hand to purchase the car debt free! Praise Jesus! Also, last year God supernaturally cancelled two of our mortgages! We are standing and believing for more debt to be paid off in Jesus' name! Thank you Jesse and Cathy. We are Partners and love your ministry and what you do for Jesus. We love your financial teachings as well.

South Dakota – Your teachings on the different types of giving in "Why Isn't My Giving Working?" and the follow-up teaching in the *Voice of the Covenant* magazine gave real clarity to us for our giving ministry. You taught us the impact of where our tithes, offerings, seed, and alms giving are going, and the care and specificity we should pay to it. We became Partners with you after Hurricane Katrina and always consider carefully the Word of God that you preach that becomes a witness to us in all that we do. What is glorious is that God is showing us every time we give into JDM, the good soil of your ministry is producing the fruit for God with souls for the Kingdom and by the meat of the Word you preach, maturity for the body of Christ. We rejoice that in these days, wherein there is so much 'trouble in the Church," you point us to the pure things of God in His Word and by the example of your lives in how you live, that the anointing of God is real upon you, and again, is a living witness for us.

Ohio – Thank you for helping the body of Christ for the past 35 years! It is greatly appreciated and God will not forget your labor of love. I want to help you help others. I have supported you with one-time gifts, or seeds as we have learned from your recent teaching, when you visit Ohio. However, after listening, reading and studying your new teaching on the four types of giving, I also want to be a monthly Partner with your ministry. I have been a born again believer for thirty years and have never heard the teaching of "giving" explained so well and broken down to understand, with the scriptures to build or support the foundation. Thank You! I am a faithful tither and sower but have always known I must be missing it somewhere. God has blessed me and been very good to me! However, I have not seen the blessings multiplied to the degree that the Word boldly states that I should—30, 60, 100-fold and even 1,000 times greater! Thanks to your expounding these truths, I expect 2013 to be my best productive year ever! With clearer understanding of "how to give," I expect God to honor His Word. I have faith to receive ALL that He has promised to His obedient children. I am willing and obedient and shall eat the Good of the Land!

Canada – Thank you for your teaching on the four types of giving. Thank you! NOW I'm giving with purpose. I look forward to being a MILLION DOLLAR GIVER TO YOUR MINISTRY.

North Carolina – I'd like to thank you for your teaching on "Why Isn't My Giving Working?" It really went off inside me! The most teaching I ever had was to tithe, and that was to go where you are fed. I've always been a giver and wondered why I wasn't gaining any ground. Now, PRAISE GOD, I know. I ask God to forgive me for being ignorant of His Word. Please pray with me that I'll do it correctly and never get it mixed up again! Your teachings have literally helped save my life. I love and appreciate you and Cathy so very much! Thank you both for being obedient to His call.

Colorado – I saw your DVD teaching about the four ways of giving. What a tremendous message! The anointing was so great on you. My Mom had been teaching me that debt is a spirit. First, I got the revelation on the spirit of debt, then cast it down and told God I don't need no stinkin' credit cards any more, I only need Him. Then I heard your message on DVD and found out about the other ways of giving and learned more about all of them. It widened my heart and sparked a desire to constantly be giving. I have been fed by your words/teachings for years. Thank you for teaching us about all kinds of stuff!

Facebook – Thank you for teaching the truth about wealth and Christianity. My husband and I grew up Baptist with a total poverty mentality. We have had three prophecies this year for great wealth and your teachings helped me receive them with greater understanding. We now have a different and quite deeper understanding, as well as for why and how the devil has robbed the church—not just financially, but also spiritually. What a tragedy!

God is good and wants to show off through His church body.

England – Thank you, Jesse, for your teaching on the four types of giving. It really impacted me. My husband and I have been tithing and giving for many years, but this truly was a revelation and the best and clearest teaching we have heard on finances.

Order this amazing message on a two-disc Special Edition DVD as a companion to the book

Over 3 hours of great teaching that will change your life forever!

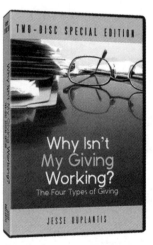

Disc 1 Includes:
- Original message by Jesse, preached at Jesse Duplantis Ministries International Headquarters in New Orleans – 60 Minutes

Disc 2 Includes:
- A supplemental message, "Why Isn't My Giving Working? The Four Types of Giving" preached by Jesse during the 2012 International Faith Conference in Chicago – 60 minutes
- An exciting sit-down Q & A session with Jesse & Cathy on The Four Types of Giving, exclusively recorded for this Two-Disc Special Edition! – 45 minutes
- A special teaching by Jesse on giving, entitled, "There are Some Things You Shouldn't Eat" (message available in this set only)

Additional Prosperity Titles by Jesse Duplantis at jdm.org

DVD Products
(Also available as digital download)

Cruise Control: The Enemy of Increase

What Do You Need? Desire? Want?

Living Off the Top of the Barrel Vol. 1

Living Off the Top of the Barrel Vol. 2

12 Ways to Achieve Total Success

The Economic Stimulus Package Before the Fall

Defining Debt and Destroying It

Taking Ownership of What is Ours (5 DVD Set)

Living Life Without Deficits

Overflow: God's Gift of Abundance for You (5 DVD Set)

When Will We Yield to the Anointing of Wealth?

God Does Not Give Big Oil to Foolish People

Fragments–Waste Not and You'll Want Not:
Your Riches are in Your Fragments

Hey! That's My Harvest!

Dirt Digging Days are Over!

The Choke Hold

CD Products
(Also available as digital download)

My Overflow is Overflowing

God's Family Plan Concerning Spiritual, Physical, and Financial Needs

God Does Not Give Big Oil to Foolish People

Look for these other books by Jesse Duplantis

Advance in Life*

The Big 12*

LIVING AT THE TOP*

For by IT...FAITH*

DISTORTION: The Vanity of Genetically Altered Christianity*

The Everyday Visionary*

What In Hell Do You Want?*

Wanting a God You Can Talk To*

Jambalaya for the Soul*

Breaking the Power of Natural Law

God Is Not Enough, He's Too Much!*

Heaven: Close Encounters of the God Kind*

The Ministry of Cheerfulness

The Sovereignty of God

Understanding Salvation
Also available in Spanish

Leave It in the Hands of a Specialist

One More Night With the Frogs

Keep Your Foot on the Devil's Neck

Running Towards Your Giant

The Battle of Life

Don't Be Affected By the World's Message

All these titles can be ordered online at www.jdm.org.
*Also available as an eBook.

To contact
Jesse Duplantis Ministries
write or call:
PO Box 1089
Destrehan, LA 70047
Phone 985.764.2000
or visit us online at
www.jdm.org

Please include your prayer request
and praise report when you write.